L.I.F.E. Line Self-Defense™

For Kids, From a Kid!

JESSIE & DAVE GERBER

Foreword by Sam Sade
Martial Arts Masters Hall of Fame

D1452257

Timeless Publishing

ISBN 978-1-943782-99-4

Timeless Publishing
www.timelesspublishing.com
info@timelesspublishing.com

Design by Gaye Newton
Photography by Robert Merhaut (www.rmp-image.com)

Printed in the United States of America

www.synergydt.com
www.davegerber.info
gerber@synergydt.com

Also by Dave Gerber

L.I.F.E. Line Self-Defense™: Kids' Ground Techniques and More!

L.I.F.E. Line Self-Defense™: Graduation, College Bound and Beyond!

L.I.F.E. Line Self Defense™: Baby Boomers and Above!

Use Conflict: Advance Your Winning Life

On Fire Leadership®: A Leader's Book of Motivational Quotes

On Fire Leadership®: Motivational Quotes for Military Leaders

On Fire Leadership®: Motivational Quotes for Martial Artists

On Fire Leadership®: Motivational Quotes for Medical Professional, Educators, and Others (coming soon)

Don't Learn the Hard Way: Pre-Marriage Questions so You Don't Get Divorced (Again)

Conquering Project Management Conflict (coming soon)

Turning $oft $kills into Hard Money: The Leader's Conflict Calculator (coming soon)

www.Synergy-Selfdefense.com
www.onfireleadershipquotes.com
www.lifelineselfdefense.com
www.kravmaga.vet
www.alphakravmaganvadc.com
www.Akminvadc.com

Important Note!

This book has been assembled, written and published strictly for informational purposes only and in no way should be used to replace or substitute actual instruction from and with qualified professionals. Jessie and I encourage everyone to learn and practice self-defense with professional coaches and instructors!

The authors and publishers of this book are providing you with knowledge and information. If you choose to act on it, at your own risk, we urge you to be aware of your or your child's health status and consult a licensed health care professional before beginning this or any similar program.

Dedication

Jessie

This book is dedicated to Oma, Buckey, Nanny Rose, my old dog, Dewey and my new dog, Freedom.

Dave

To Howie Osterer.

For the people of all ages who had an adult tell them they couldn't do something and overcame it anyway. To the people who were told that their ideas weren't good enough but kept working and made it happen. To all the kids and adults who turned doubters into believers. To the kids and adults who have fought through challenges and pushed their limits to new heights. To all kids everywhere, who have the right to know how to defend themselves.

Never give up!

"An aware parent loves all children he or she interacts with,
for you are a caretaker for those moments in time."
~ Doc Childre

Acknowledgements

Jessie

Some of the people I want to say thank you to for supporting me in my life and in this project are my Dad, my Mom, Gigi, Papa, Grammy, Rowpa and Glenda. I also want to acknowledge my friends—Elena, Addison and McKenna—and my past, current and future teachers. I especially want to thank all of the kids, younger and older than me, who have supported me with this book and in life. A special thank you to my Dad for including me in this book and the other one, because it means so much to me, and I love you.

Dave

I want to acknowledge how much I enjoyed doing this project with Jessie. She is an incredible daughter and it is so great both to love and truly like your child, too. Choosing to work from home to be a major factor in raising Jessie since birth has been a priceless choice for the two of us, as we have an awesome relationship.

Next, having a great friend and mentor, Sam Sade, who has truly supported this part of my life journey is so meaningful. Having a great support network of friends and AKMI family members that are truly caring has been extremely meaningful. Their technical skill and knowledge are the very best available.

I would like to thank the progressive leaders who want to change the world by thinking holistically about a child's needs, including self-defense.

I would also like to acknowledge those who fight in our military to protect our freedom, those who have served and the family members of those who have served. Thank you.

Lastly, I would also like to acknowledge and thank all of the instructors, coaches and colleagues I have had throughout the years (and those I will meet in the future), both from the US, Israel and more. Thank you to those individuals who are always willing to teach me, because they know I am always willing to learn.

"So we may walk in peace."
~ Imi Lichtenfeld, founder of Krav Maga

Special Testimonials

"I love working with kids at my Systems Training Centers, and they love learning Self-Defense and Krav Maga, so I know children everywhere will love it! I am impressed with Dave's ability to understand, capture and share these concepts in a book that is so meaningful to anyone that has kids. Everyone needs to read this book, including parents, as it can help with having good discussions about real world conflict and the need to be able to take care of yourself in all ways, including safety. Also worthy of praise are Dave's efforts as a leadership and conflict management consultant, trainer, coach and motivational speaker. He has intertwined his education from different specialty areas to create a special contribution to the national community. His passion is electric, and you can feel that when you hold and read this book. Nice job, Dave and Jessie!"

~ Marcus Kowal
   Parent, 2nd Dan Black Belt in Krav Maga, Coach/Instructor of multiple Marital Arts,
   Professional Fighter, Systems Training Center Owner

"All parents and kids need to read this book, together and on their own! Dave has captured the essence of self-defense and given it back to us in a manner everyone can understand and appreciate. Including his daughter is also amazing, and to hear her voice throughout the book was effective and fun. The excellent pictures made everything come to life. The entire nation will look at self-defense differently. My daughter and I have looked through it many times! I know kids everywhere, and adults, are going to love it!"

~ Melanie Smith
   2nd Degree Black Belt in Patriot Martial Arts blended system

"Dave Gerber is one of the most passionate and skilled instructors of Krav Maga you will ever meet. His enthusiasm for helping people learn to protect themselves is amazing, and his energy is contagious. There are a lot of complicated self-defense books out there, but Dave delivers a clear and simple message in his training books. I highly recommend this book!!"

~ Master Chun Rhee
   The Legendary Jhoon Rhee TKD

"At my Rockstar Martial Arts Gym, we train females five and up, and many of them, whatever their age, are new to self-defense. More and more women are joining us looking to learn as much as possible so they can walk through life more empowered. For that reason alone, I know they will deeply value Dave's book, just like women around the country. The fact that he included his daughter is awesome. This book provides two things society needs now for girls—knowing how to protect themselves from any potential violence and parents being able to talk to their daughters about it before they graduate and leave their home. This book is that bridge! Parents and their kids will love this book. These skills are great for women of any age as well! Great job, Dave!"

> ~John Tiano
> Parent, 6th Dan Black Belt, Owner of Rockstar Martial Arts, Boston, Massachusetts Area

"As a female instructor of martial arts, I feel it is necessary for every young woman to have the knowledge and ability to defend herself in a potentially threatening situation. The contents in this book and Dave Gerber's seminars teaches the core components of self-defense—simple and fast maneuvers with the mindset to do them quickly and effectively."

> ~ Master Jackie Curiel
> 4th Dan Jhoon Rhee Institute of TKD, over 20 years of martial arts experience

"Self-defense is 90 percent mental and 10 percent physical. To survive in any self-defense situation, the defender must be smarter than the attacker. This book provides the basics with great photos, skills and inspiration to families. It will absolutely help kids learn more about what to do if faced with a dangerous situation, and parents will enjoy reading it with them. Excellent read."

> ~ Bert Witte
> 3rd Degree Black Belt, Alpha Krav Maga, 5th Degree Black Belt, Degerberg International Martial Arts, 6th Degree Black Belt, Bu Kyoku Ryu Karate

"You feel the energy when you pick up the book…even more when you hand it to someone you care about. Thank you, Dave, for being a strong, supportive ally for empowering girls and women of all ages to protect themselves anywhere and everywhere they go! Dave Gerber's programs and this book are game changers!"

> ~ Diana Azrikam
> Black Belt, Alpha Krav Maga and Instructor

"Dave is one of the most passionate, fun, professional, energizing, motivating coaches you will ever meet. His students not only love learning Krav Maga and self-defense, they love his approach towards relationships, learning and life. His background in education, conflict management, leadership and self-defense all blend well for an excellent gift to the international community. Every family should own a copy of this and his other L.I.F.E. Line Self-Defense books, too. You will truly enjoy them."

> ~ George Buruian
> Martial Arts Masters Hall of Fame

"As a mother of a ten-year-old daughter, I feel that every girl should own this book! Raising awareness with training and programs like this are a part of being more prepared for life and are essential. Society is getting more dangerous. Learning self-defense is crucial. Dave has put together an empowering, extremely helpful and straightforward guide to the basics for how girls can protect themselves. I highly recommend this book, as I teach the very same skills and know they save lives!"

> ~ Bernadette Ambubuyog
> Black Belt, Krav Maga and Instructor

"What Dave has written here is what all parents need to address. Let's face it, we can't be everywhere in order to protect our children. We must empower them to handle what life throws at them. Teaching them the verbal and physical skills is necessary. I highly recommend this for all parents."

> ~ Derek Randel
> Author of *The Stopping School Violence Manual* and *Attacking our Educators*

"At Roy Elghanayan's Krav Maga (aka Krav Maga LA), we start implementing self-defense foundational skills to three year olds. Just like the skills we share at our school, Dave Gerber has put together a treasured guide for kids everywhere. I highly suggest that anyone with kids gets a copy! This book will change the way you think about your child's safety and your own, too. Really well done, educating pictures and fun to read. This is a great contribution to the self-defense and larger community."

> ~ Roy Elghanayan
> 4th Dan Black Belt Krav Maga, Owner and Head Coach REKM in LA

Testimonials from Parents

"In a word, Awesome! In more words, every parent, grandparent and child needs to read this book, now."

~ Joan R.

"Dave Gerber is a fantastic coach and is totally committed to people learning about the L.I.F.E. Line Self-Defense Program, as you will see in this awesome new book he put together for kids and women of all ages! When working with people of all kinds, he always makes sure he does this in a positive and empowering way. He has tremendous ability and enthusiasm for helping people be aware of how to be positive, more aware of their surroundings and their personal safety. Dave stands out from the other coaches. We know personally, because our daughter trains with him."

~ Stephanie and Marc

"This is book incredible. I have known Dave for several years and have seen his motivational teaching style that is so energetic, fun and effective. The last class I saw him teach elements of L.I.F.E. Line, there were girls (and others) from ages eight to 78. One of the most engaging coaches I have ever met, he is also funny and sure to put a smile on your face. He loves helping people, period. The fact that he created this book with Jessie is so awesome. The kids at our Patriot Martial Arts gym love Dave's classes and we know this book is going to be a huge hit for children and families everywhere!"

~ Juanita H., Parent, Blue Sash Instructor in Malay Eskrima

"My husband and I are so happy you put this together. We are telling every parent we know! Thank you Jessie and Dave!"

~ Diane and Charlie S.

"Adults teach their kids how to do chores, clean themselves, learn, drive, and be a good citizen…they also need to learn self-defense before leaving home. Really well done, easy to follow. In fact I enjoyed it myself before even showing it to the kids!"

~ Tim N.

"We all know bullying is an issue. Just like you can't expect 911 to teleport or show up instantly to save you on the streets, kids can't expect an adult to be there who will step in immediately. Now adults are getting in trouble for trying to help, too. I want my daughter to be able help herself. This book is just what our children, parents, schools and communities needed. Thank you!"

~ Jason R.

"There is a difference between a martial arts and self-defense. Martial arts is good for kids, and they need to know self-defense too. The bad guy is a real attacker and not looking to score points. This is about knowing your kids can escape and survive. Thank you."

~ Connie B.

"This is the perfect resource at the perfect time for our kids. They need to know we support them and give them permission to strike an adult that is trying to hurt them or take them away. Kids are taught not to hit and that is good. But, if it comes down to life, death or being taken I want our kids to fight and escape every time."

~ Rich V.

Praise from Kids

For L.I.F.E. Line Self-Defense training programs with Coach Dave

"I am now very confident and I feel less vulnerable and more powerful. This was a great experience. Jessie was great too!"

"More prepared, less scared, confident. I feel better prepared for real life situations. I want to tell others what I learned and would come again to learn more."

"I really liked learning and practicing the techniques. My favorite part was the fake fight (red man), because I could apply the techniques and I liked dealing with the adrenaline rush. It feels good knowing I can defend myself."

"Fun. It was great! I know some techniques and skills needed to defend myself."

"Loved the talking, empowerment portion, talk on bullying."

"I learned a lot of useful stuff I can use in the future to help me be more safe, thanks!"

"He made the skills easy to learn but still fun and challenging. We learned lots of different defenses, not just one."

"Everything was about defense, not attacking or starting a confrontation."

"The class made me feel a little bit safer, especially if something bad happens."

"I learned a lot of useful information, and the demonstrations showed how the skills were not hard to perform."

"I thought that the mentality of raising awareness, your life is worth it and your life is on the line is important! And I think that it is great men and women now can really benefit from these types of classes. Thank you."

Training with Dave

"Awesome, every girl and woman should take this program as Dave empowers you and teaches you great, practical skills that can be used immediately!"

"Take this program. It may save your life and/or help you protect your family!"

"I'm so glad my daughter has been through this program!"

"Dave, this is what I needed and it immediately helped me for when I have to deal with my ex!"

"I realized what I didn't know and have started empowering myself with awesome skills, thanks!"

"What every woman should know, Dave explains situations, response moves in a way that is easy to understand and fun!"

"Great teacher! Dave takes something serious and makes it fun!"

"Very positive, upbeat and practical. You can learn a lot in a short amount of time."

"Do it!! Fight the Redman and practice in this class rather than do it on the street first."

"It's really fun and you actually learn a lot. I feel confident. Dave is very good at teaching."

"Dave is very passionate and energetic about this. You can tell he truly cares and is good."

"Dave takes something serious and makes it fun."

Foreword

By Sam Sade
Martial Arts Masters Hall of Fame, 4th Dan Black Belt in Krav Maga
Owner of Alpha Krav Maga International
and Parent

Growing up in a rough neighborhood as a kid forced me to learn how to defend myself, as trouble always found people trying to do good. As a result, I was forced to teach myself the "ways of the streets." It wasn't until after my time as a weight lifter and winning the Mr. Israel competition two times that I discovered that my skills were a great foundation to what would become my first black belt in Krav Maga, earned in only two and a half years. It is because of my hard work and natural gift that I am able to share that with thousands of people around the world, helping to empower them in their own lives to be the best they can be. These students, new and old, empower me as well, and with their energy, I continue to teach as much as possible.

It is a fantastic experience to be a part of a project that could potentially help so many kids, parents and their families. Dave and Jessie have taken the initiative and are showing great leadership and love for people with this book. From the beginning, I have also been impressed with his humility and desire to learn and grow and share as a Krav Maga Coach *and* Practitioner. Dave has only the best of intentions in his heart, and he was born to be a teacher, a coach, and a leader. As I heard him say one time, he would describe himself in four words: teacher, healer, warrior, and poet. He is, without question, what he aims to be. He does it with true passion, courage and sense of purpose.

Jessie is an amazing girl who continues to impress people every time they see her. It is so great to see this "Daddy-Daughter Duo." They represent the Krav Maga and Self-Defense community with great integrity. Dave and Jessie have created a great project for their legacies together and as individuals!

Even though children are taught not to hit, especially adults, there have to be exceptions when defending themselves. It is important that parents give their children permission to strike when their safety and life are on the line! This books helps provide that permission.

Table of Contents

Chapter 1: Introduction

Jessie

This is really exciting. I am so happy that my Dad and I did these two book projects. It is so cool! He always says, "wisdom not shared is wisdom wasted." So we decided to put this book together for kids, together. We worked on the all parts of the book, especially the photographs, and we both comment throughout the book. We used each other's strengths to make a good project for the world. My Dad asked my opinions on different parts of the book from beginning to end. He did most of the work putting it together, but he included me a lot. The entire time he asked me if things were good. I am really proud of us, and I think his idea to help kids, and adults too, with L.I.F.E. Line Self-Defense is awesome.

So my Dad came to me one day and told me that we could write a book together on self-defense based upon work he has been doing and creating. For his job, as long as I have been alive, he has been working with and training leaders and all kinds of companies on conflict, communication and leadership issues. For the last six years, he has also been able to study self-defense very intensely. He became a coach after training with some of the best coaches in the Krav Maga world, especially Sam Sade. By the way, Sam is an awesome guy, not just great at Krav Maga ☺.

My Dad is a former high school teacher, coach and camp counselor. (Actually, he did all of that before I was even born, ha!) Now he has been working in the field of helping people and businesses lead and communicate better so people can be nicer to one another at work, and so they can have less conflict. But he always missed working with students, so he came up with an idea: L.I.F.E. Line.

My Dad came up with the L.I.F.E. Line Self Defense system, which he teaches to kids and adults of all kinds from all different backgrounds. I have helped him as his favorite student ☺. He made this book project about self-defense because he wanted to make an easy "how to" book to help us kids (but I keep telling him it is for adults too!). He realized that a lot of times, kids would rather listen to other kids than adults. So he asked me if I wanted to be involved with the books and blend our voices together and make a cool project to remember forever. I want to help other kids feel more comfortable and powerful in their own bodies. They are for everyone, every size, shape and level of conditioning. These skills are for self-defense only.

The two hardest parts about this are learning the moves and being aggressive, like the picture of me on the cover of this book. Truly we are nice people, and we don't want to hurt anyone. Well my dad and I made this book so you can learn the moves to go with your training. If someone really wants to hurt us or take us away, we might have to hurt them, even if that is not our normal personality.

What I know is I want to go home safe to my parents and my dog Freedom and my family and my friends. I want to be better prepared for living a happy life, more aware, have the ability to fight a bad guy if I have to and escape away from the danger, if it is near school or out in society. I am happy my Dad is teaching people how to better deal with problems at their jobs *and* now teaching people how to deal with danger. While we are not teaching every move you need to know, there are a lot of them in here which are really helpful. We put together a second book to help you if you're on the ground and more.

I hope you like this book, because we made it with you in mind, hoping you would like it and tell your friends, because everyone needs to be safe. The pictures were so cool to make and I know you will think they are helpful. Please don't use this information to hurt your brothers or sisters or family members or schoolmates or anyone unless you think you are in real danger. It is also really important, and my dad talks about this all the time, to be really safe when training. These skills need to be practiced when under control. It isn't good if anyone gets hurt and you feel bad. Both my dad and I say, "please be safe!"

Consider this before we start:

1. Would you climb through a tunnel filled with disgusting trash, worms, yucky water that stunk to make it home to your parents?
2. Would you eat an apple with flies on it if it was the only way to go home to your family and loved ones?
3. Do you think these questions are "gross?"

Well the truth is the answer to question #1 and #2 is yes, obviously. Wouldn't you agree? Yes, gross! Well some of the techniques that we have to do in self-defense might be called gross too, but we would do them if it was the only way we could go home safely to our parents, families, friends and pets. While it is not the same, I would change my personality from being my usual nice self to doing whatever I had to do to get home safely. When you think about it, wouldn't you?

Thank you for reading this book, and I hope you can see the other book my Dad and I made to help when people are dealing with attacks while on the ground and maybe someone on top of you in a worst case situation. Also, we want to share more so you can find some videos of the techniques online soon. Thank you and I hope to meet you in person one day!

Dave

Wow! How cool, and what a great introduction. My love for my daughter and other kids is the main reason I wrote this book. As you will see, I have blended our two voices throughout the project.

To write two self-defense books with my daughter with the hopes of helping all kids learn how to be safer, to feel more empowered and expand their potential is an awesome experience. While we have not included anywhere near all of the techniques needed to be completely safe (not to mention real practice), we feel it is just right for what and how much kids want to learn to get started. It is written with the understanding that kids have less strength and body weight than an adult. This book is meant to help make self-defense more of a focused, natural response to danger.

The reality is we grow and raise our kids (right kids? Right parents?). We teach them how to clean themselves, do their homework and chores, handle responsibilities, drive, vote, and be prepared for life after they leave school and our homes. We may realize we forgot to help them learn how to keep their physical bodies safe! Then what?

This book was put together for all the reasons Jessie mentioned above in her introduction. It is my goal to help *everyone* learn how to protect themselves. Hopefully this book is motivational for you, as a kid, to learn more and practice with professionals. Hopefully it is motivational for parents to put these books in their kids' hands and talk to them about the related issues. It is a win-win-win for kids, parents, and society.

It was great working with Jessie to create the photographs that helped to explain everything better, too. My feeling was that kids would rather see and learn from a kid, and Jessie really loves to help people learn, too.

I hope to train with you at some point in the future at a class, seminar, camp or any other program we create together! I believe kids can do far more than many adults ever can imagine. I've seen it, and I continue to watch Jessie and other kids do just that! I'm glad to be a part of the solution with you.

With love and respect,
Never give up! Never!

Dave

Chapter 2: What is L.I.F.E. Line Self-Defense™?

L.I.F.E. Line Self-Defense uses an acronym to provide a simple way of thinking or approach about life from the perspective of self-defense. L.I.F.E. Line stands for Listen (to your) Intuition, Fight, and Escape.

LISTEN

INTUITION

FIGHT

ESCAPE

The L.I.F.E. Line Self-Defense System

The L.I.F.E. Line Self-Defense System is all about living positively, being more aware of surroundings and getting home to loved ones by being more prepared, not scared. Not fighting, but escaping! However, if you have to fight to survive or defend yourself, it is important to know what and how to do it.

Important Note!

This book has been assembled, written and published strictly for informational purposes only and in no way should be used to replace or substitute actual instruction from and with qualified professionals. Jessie and I encourage everyone to learn and practice self-defense with professional coaches and instructors!

The authors and publishers of this book are providing you with knowledge and information. If you choose to act on it, at your own risk, we urge you to be aware of your or your child's health status and consult a licensed health care professional before beginning this or any similar program.

Listen

Some thoughts connected to Listen include:
- Listening is about using all of your senses, not just your ears. They all work together.
- Listen to your parents, teachers, and those around you who want you to succeed.
- Hear what people are saying. Don't just brush off important details.
- Listen the environment and look for clues.
- Listen to animals (dogs growling, birds flying away, etc.). They often sense danger before we do.
- Understand that you are a problem solver and that force is a last resort. The more you train, the better decisions you can make.
- Listen to others and be helpful. Be a force for good, and think about how you can make the world a better place.
- Behind every complaint is a request. Listen for what people really want.
- Bring forth positive energy, love of self and respect for others.
- Care for your classmates and community members, and listen to people's needs.
- Believe in reflection and self-improvement. Trust yourself and those who truly care for you.
- Discard those things and spend less time around people that do not support you.
- Remember peer pressure is real. You have to learn how to manage it positively while not pressuring others.
- Respect and represent your family and your parents in the best way possible.

Intuition

The "I" or Intuition is about:
- Trust your gut feelings!
- Listen to your body/mind connection and your feelings.
- Report bullying and cyber-bullying when you see it or experience it to your parents and school.
- Don't be scared, be prepared and then share. When we are more prepared for anything, we are less nervous and more open to the good things the universe has to offer. We need to share our plans with others so they know where we are in case something happens.
- Learn to defend yourself. You will be less afraid as you grow up in this very large world. If you are prepared you do not have to get ready if something bad happens.
- Understand that when you leave your house, you leave the place where you have control.
- Pay attention to what's around you. Learn about your environment.
- If it doesn't feel right, it probably isn't.
- Most bad things and poor decisions happen from 3:00 pm to 5:00 pm and after 10:00 pm.
- Consider your peer group and make it positive.
- Make safe decisions when out. Don't walk alone in unfamiliar places, and always share your plans with friends and family.
- Never get in the car with anyone who you think has the desire to harm you. Fight, fight, fight!

Fight

When it comes to the "Fight," we use self-defense techniques from the best system, Krav Maga. We also realize the goal is really to get to "E," Escape, as fast as possible. But if we have to fight to save ourselves, we have to do anything and everything possible. The pictures and descriptions in following chapters are based on Krav Maga principles that are taught in many systems. While we believe Alpha Krav Maga International offers the best system and great people, many systems in Krav Maga use these basic self-defense skills.

We believe the three most important things to remember are:
- Explosive power
- Focused strike points on the attacker's body
- Never give up! Never!

Many people who fight back do not strike fast or to the right places on the body that do the most damage. Remember, we need to stun them and escape. In one chapter, we will discuss the body parts to use and places to strike on the bad guy, even before getting into any skills or techniques.

Escape

The "E" in L.I.F.E. Line stands for "Escape." This is about how we yell, bite, scream, scratch, hit, kick, stomp or do whatever we can to get up and get away. We also yell and scream during the "Fight" part of L.I.F.E. to distract and startle. Noise and being loud are very important, and we never want to be on the ground! However, as we are trying to run away, we might end up there. So we need to know how to fight and get away when on our back (check out our other book for a few of those skills). We want to go home to our loved ones, so we only fight so that we can escape. This is self-defense, not boxing or mixed martial arts like many adults watch on TV.

Why Use the Krav Maga Techniques?

Because they work the best, period. Krav Maga uses the best techniques taught in other systems and is the best of all systems when it comes to removing a threat from a bad guy or girl as quickly as possible. Krav Maga means "close contact" in Hebrew, so the entire system is meant to help when the person is "in your face" and threating to hurt you or take you away, or has actually attacked you. The goal is to end it and get away as fast as possible. The system is based upon natural movements of the body, so it is easy to learn. But only practice and training will help you feel prepared.

The founder of Krav Maga was Imi Lichtenfeld. You can read a lot about him online. He was a great and important man that had to teach people, of all kinds, how to defend themselves when Israel started as a country in 1948 after the Holocaust (you can learn about that when your parents think you are ready.) Krav Maga is now taught all over the world to people of all kinds. We encourage you to look more into the background and history of Krav Maga to get a better appreciation of what you are learning. These self-defense techniques work.

Where does Bullying Fit into This Discussion?

There are a lot of resources, online and beyond, on this subject about prevention, management and resolution. I have taught courses to educators and have a great deal of experience and content knowledge on the subject of bullying. For this book, let's consider some questions for kids and parents to talk about together so they can be more informed about their own environment:

- What is written in the school code of conduct or handbook about bullying and cyber-bullying?
- What are the rules discussed with students about bullying?
- What is the current level of enforcement of those rules?
- How are bullying situations resolved? For instance, is some version of "Restorative Practices" used to create closure?
- What strategies to prevent, manage and resolve bullying are expected of your kids? And adults?
- What system of reporting exists for bullying?
- What support system is needed for all of the people involved?
- What are the rules around self-defense?
- Does law enforcement need to be involved?
- How does the L.I.F.E. Line model of self-defense fit into your last resort options?

This is not anywhere near a complete list of questions. However for this project, we just want people to consider that bullying goes unaddressed often gets violent. If bullying gets violent, kids need to be prepared to defend themselves. There is no time to learn to get ready when it is taking place. The L.I.F.E. Line method of thinking about self-defense stresses violence as a last resort. If you are being bullied or know someone who is, tell an adult immediately to get the support you need!

Coach Daddy Dave: What are your favorite parts about the L.I.F.E. Line System that we are sharing with everyone?

Jessie: It's awesome to help other kids learn more about how to live more safely and be prepared in case something were to happen. I know it probably won't, but I want to be prepared to take care of my own body in case no one is around to help me. I imagine helping others by throwing a lifeline from a boat. We're really helping families talk about these issues.

Coach Daddy Dave: Is there anything you want kids to remember in particular about the L.I.F.E. Line Self-Defense system we are talking about?

Jessie: It's easy and it makes sense. It's fun to learn, and it works! We have to be able to help ourselves if no one is around.

Chapter 3: Body Parts and Targets

> **Coach Daddy Dave:** Jessie, how do you feel about training knowing that you could poke an attacker's eyes or their throat and hurt them?
>
> **Jessie:** I don't want to hurt anyone, period. The only reason I would have to is if someone was trying to hurt me. Because this is not a martial art and you don't get points, everything goes when it comes to going home safely.
>
> **Coach Daddy Dave:** Do you think this thinking is okay?
>
> **Jessie:** Of course, dad. If someone is trying to hurt me, I am going home to you and mom and my family and my friends and my dog no matter what I have to do, even if I have to punch or kick or whatever.

So when dealing with "stranger danger" bad guys or girls, attackers, or people that want to be violent to us, the key is to use parts of our own body that are hard and to connect them with soft parts of attacker's body. Eyes, ears and the throat are just a few examples.

In this section, we will demonstrate pictures to show you what parts of our body we want to use when striking. Later in the chapter, we will show you the "focused strike points" or "targets" on the attacker that will do the most damage with the least amount of effort. These are techniques only done when in danger or when being attacked so we can get away.

It is important to remember that we want to use "hard" parts of the body so we are less likely to hurt ourselves and more likely to stun/injure the bad person. It is also important to remember that what we are showing is only one moment in time. We don't know why or how someone ends up in specific bad situation. Maybe they could have done something different in the seconds before, maybe, maybe, maybe. There is no way for any teacher to answer every question or "what if," because there are too many. Combinations, of all types and strikes, should be used to defend ourselves and quickly get away.

Using Your Body Parts for Striking

In the following pictures you will see the parts of our body we use when striking a soft target area (part of the bad guy/girl's body) so we can escape:

Bone at bottom of palm under pinky to all targets (Palm Strikes)

When punching, top two knuckles only (recommend palm strikes instead)

Portion above, the point, or immediately below the elbow

Bottom muscle portion of hand when making a fist (Hammer Fist)

Fingers together, slightly bent and stiff wrist for eye gouges

Above, not on, the knee cap for knee strikes

Stiff wrist to mid forearm for inside defenses

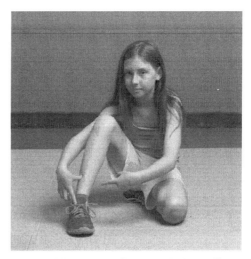

Top of foot to shin for groin kicks, stiff ankle, toes pointed down

Outside bony part of arms for outside defense

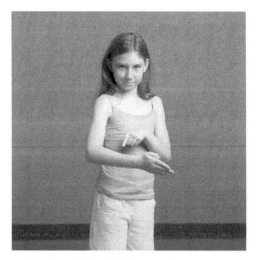

Palm to mid, inside forearm for groin strikes

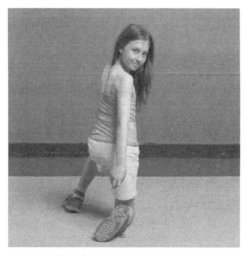

Heel of foot for stomp kicks

Body Parts to Target on the Attacker

Now that we know what to parts of our body to use, we need to consider what targets we strike on the bad guy. We are fearing for our safety and defending ourselves. We don't want to hurt this person, but they are trying or planning to hurt us. So we have to quickly strike the following areas so that we can escape even if they get hurt or even bleed. Hey, they are the bad ones, not us.

Ears, eyes, throat, nose and groin are the best targets because we strike with a "boney" part of our body to a soft part of the attacker's body. In the pictures below, you will see where on the body we strike. The benefit of striking these parts on the attacker is to better ensure they stop in time for us to escape. Don't forget to yell and make a lot of noise! ("You're not my dad!" "Help!" "Police!" "Stranger danger!")

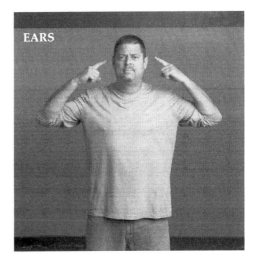

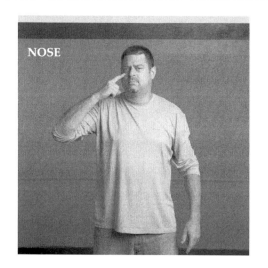

NOSE

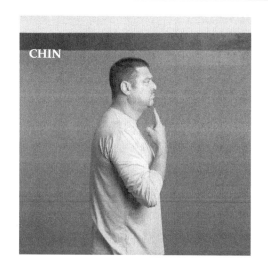

CHIN

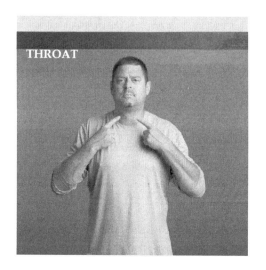

THROAT

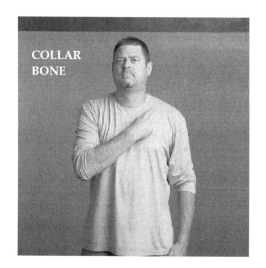

COLLAR BONE

GROIN

KNEE

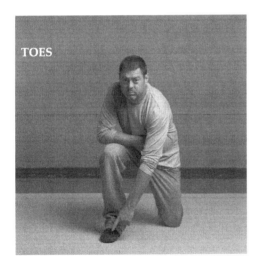

TOES

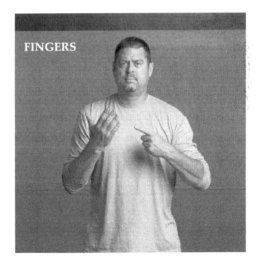

FINGERS

Chapter 4: Standing, Moving, Self-Defense Stance

Standing

"Standing" is just that—we are standing in a normal, everyday, passive position. A "Self-Defense Stance" is a position we learn. We feel comfortable and safer, ready for anything to happen, even if we don't let the bad person know we are in the Self-Defense Stance. Look at the positions below to see how Jessie is just standing. Then looking at her Self-Defense Stance. We all have to be able to go from a regular stance to a Self-Defense Stance in an instant!

Coach Daddy Dave: What would you like people to remember as really important from your teachings about your Self-Defense Stance?

Jessie: It's all about balance. You don't want someone to be able to push you down from any direction.

Coach Daddy Dave: Is there anything else?

Jessie: Yes, a good stance is important because you have to have your hands up to defend yourself, and you want to have good balance if you need to block and defend. A good stance equals better movement.

Remember, Make A Lot of Noise!

If we think someone is trying to hurt us, remember, if we can be loud, scream, use our voice to draw attention to us, the bad guy might even run away. We don't stop yelling if we are being attacked; people all over need to hear us!

"Scream and yell all kinds of things like, 'Stop! Get away! You're not my dad! Help me!'" Jessie says.

Our Self-Defense Stance is important, as it gives us balance and helps us to move. Our feet are staggered, one foot forward and the other back to provide balance, just a little past shoulder width apart. We have to be prepared to be pushed from all sides. We are on the balls of our feet.

Notice how this stance allows Jessie to be more balanced and prepared. She can let the person know she doesn't want trouble. She can start yelling and attracting attention now, too! ~ Dave

We have our hands up, fingers and thumb tight, wrists stiff, our elbows bent so our hand are out in front. We keep our hands up at all times in this position, so we are prepared to block (see that chapter coming up).

Moving

Moving is very important, but it first starts with our balance, like mentioned above. As in our Self-Defense Stance, we are grounded to the floor and cannot be pushed over from any side. At the same time, we have to be able to pick up our feet and move and turn to face the bad guy or girl in any direction. We use the opposite foot to push off, so we can move without crossing our feet over (we don't want to trip).

But our front and back feet in this Self-Defense Stance are always on the "ball of the foot" or the area before our toes, solidly attached to the ground. We may lift our heel slightly. "But be stable and planted on the ground," says Jessie.

So if we want to go to the left, we push off with our right foot. If we want to go to the right, we push off with our left foot. If we want to go forward, we push off with our back foot. If we want to go backwards, we push off our front foot. It may seem simple, but it takes a lot of practice, especially if we want to maintain our balance 100 percent of the time.

If we want to turn, we take a step with our front foot in the direction we want to go and then bring our back foot with us so that we can put it down in our same balanced Self-Defense Stance, facing the threat.

In the example below, Jessie exaggerates the motion:

In the first picture, I am in my Self-Defense Stance. In the next picture above, I pushed off my back foot and am stepping left with my front foot. In the bottom picture, I pushed off my front foot and am stepping back. ~ Jessie

Chapter 5: Blocking

Coach Daddy Dave: What is one major thing you remember about blocking?

Jessie: (laughing) I always remember you say that Coach George (George Buruian, an AKMI Coach in Chicago) says, "protect your coconut." (Still laughing and putting her hands near her head)

Coach Daddy Dave: You're funny. What else do you have to say?

Jessie: (Serious face) Seriously…protect your coconut. When you think bad things may happen you want to have your hands up because things happen fast. You need your head for everything, and because punches move so fast, our hands must be up at all times.

Even before blocking, we recommend the option to yell and run, as we've said before. Most attackers cannot run 100 to 150 yards, as they are simply out of shape. We yell and run to get help!

That said, we think it is important to know how to block a punch or strike to the face or body before learning how to strike back. Sometimes the block is so good, the bad guy or girl goes right by or they hurt themselves. Blocking consists of "Inside Defenses" and "Outside Defenses."

When we do Inside Defense, whether we are in a regular stance or not, we are really protecting the face, throat and head area. When we do Outside Defense, we are blocking strikes (not with anything hard like a bat as those threats have different defenses) that start from outside the body and are directed anywhere.

Inside Defenses

Inside Defenses are made using a stiff wrist, fingers extended and together, slightly bent. We use the inside of our forearm to block, from middle of our palm to the middle of our forearm. We actually redirect the punch so it "slides" by as opposed to trying to put our hand in front of the punch to stop it.

It only takes a small motion to re-direct the punch. Be sure your hands are up at all times, and expect more than one punch. Keep blocking until you get a good chance to strike back. But don't wait too long; you may not block everything. ~ Jessie

Outside Defenses

For our blocks in this book, Outside Defenses are done with a stiff wrist, fingers extended and together, slightly bent. We block with the bony part of the outside of our forearm.

These punches can come from any direction and are intended to go around our raised hands, usually to strike our head. When our hands are up, we can block using our natural reflexes and good technique.

We want to block it as early as possible so it is less likely to hit us. With outside defense, we are actually stopping the strike. ~ Jessie

More Blocks

Knowing how to block a hook punch or threat that we see at the last minute that gets beyond our Outside Defense block is important. The best thing to do is reach back and grab the back of our head to cover the sensitive areas of the side or our throat, neck, head and back of head (very, very important areas of the body to protect).

In the picture above, Jessie makes the block early. In the picture to the left, she see it at the last minute and grabs to the back of her head to cover sensitive areas.
~ Dave

Chapter 6: Striking

Unfortunately if we have to block, we may have to strike back so we can get away and move to "E" for escape. However, if we are forced to defend ourselves, we do whatever we have to do. When we say strike, we mean kick, palm strike, hammer fist, knee, elbows—essentially hitting and kicking!

Do animals fight and try to hurt other animals? Of course they do. Humans are the only animals that have the ability to know they are animals but deny or don't think of it this way every day. Of course we are "animals" of sorts, and so it is not surprising, like a cat might fight another cat, a human might try to hurt another human. Hitting back may be our only and last option.

Coach Daddy Dave: So Jessie, what are your thoughts on hitting?

Jessie: Well, it's kind of funny because you always taught me not to hit when I was a baby and little kid. Teeth are not meant for biting, hands are not for hitting, and now you are saying different. *But* I get it. This is about when in danger. So I feel good about it knowing that I will probably never need it but am more prepared. These skills make me feel powerful. I also like being nice and friendly.

Coach Daddy Dave: How do you know when to start hitting?

Jessie: Well, I wouldn't hit unless someone tried to hit me and I couldn't solve it any other way or if I thought someone was going to grab me to hurt me or take me away in a car. But if it was someone trying to hurt me, I might hit first because I don't have as much strength as bigger people.

Coach Daddy Dave: Do you think you could do it?

Jessie: I know I could do it. You showed me how—you just turn it on like a light switch then turn it off and go back to being nice.

There are several types of strikes such as eye and throat gouges, punches (not always recommended), palm strikes, hammer fists, and elbows. We can even hit a shoulder to help us get away. All of these can cause severe damage, so it must be last resort of self-defense only.

Power Comes From the Hips

Before looking at the different types of strikes, it is important to remember that with each one of them, power comes from the hips! People think it comes from the arms or hands, but is the hips that give the extra power needed. All can be done without moving hips, especially if we are unable to for some reason (like being lifted), yet it is better to know that real power comes from this part of our body.

In a self-defense position, when we "strike" or "hit," our hips move in a push-pull motion. If you imagine a line running down the side of each pant leg, when we punch, for example, that line goes from facing to the left or right to facing forward. Whichever hand we strike with, our hips are turned. Think of a clock. If our left leg is forward and our left hip is facing nine o'clock, when we punch it will now be facing 12 o'clock. Just for a second, remember, our hips are a push-pull motion and our arms go in and out fast. Think of reaching into the refrigerator and grabbing something as fast as you can and pulling your arm out before it closed on you.

Look at the photos below about hip motion and turn, then see what it looks like with a palm strike as an example.

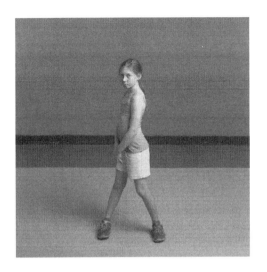

While Jessie can do a palm strike without moving her hips, it will not have as much power. See how her hip rotation looks with and without a strike, in this case a palm strike. ~ Dave

Wrist Grabs

As mentioned earlier, hip rotation is critical. Even before striking, we may have to get free from the bad guy or girl. If we can escape without striking, we run! One technique we need to know that includes hip movement is a wrist grab defense. Someone might walk by us, reach out, grab our wrist and say, "Hey, let's walk over here." If we feel uncomfortable with the way that person is grabbing our wrist, whether they are using two hands or one, we should consider the following techniques below:

In the first set of pictures, only one of Jessie's wrists is grabbed. She immediately moves her elbow toward her belly button while moving her thumb over her shoulder. Notice she also takes a step back with her leg to move her body out of the way. The key to getting free is to "break the buckle," or release her own hand by pulling it through the bad guy's hand, where his thumb and finger meet.

In the second set of pictures, Jessie has two hands around one of her wrists. First she makes a fist, reaches over top and grabs her own fist. As she pulls it our fast, she steps back with one leg. She can then run or strike with palm strikes, hammer fist punches or kicks. ~ Dave

Strikes (Hitting, Kicking and More)

Unfortunately some dangerous threats may require us to strike to get home safely. So now that we know how to move our hips, and we have to hit back, let's talk about the different strikes. The reality is that the self-defense techniques are often very effective and can cause serious damage. Just as safety in training is important, determining whether we want to do any particular technique is a choice we have to make in the moment. If it is an attacker, we do everything we can and use every skill.

We must understand that blood and other physical responses to receiving a strike may happen. We have to be ready. If we are not ready to see blood when we hit a bad guy or girl in the nose, we are not ready. If we are not ready for this, we may freeze and be unable to escape. The person may be able to recover and grab us again. No one can make choices for anyone else in the moment about what is right for them. Training and practice will help a lot. Making these types of decisions takes preparation.

So here we goooo…

Scratching and Biting

"First, what does a cat do when it is under attack? It uses its claws to scratch and it bites," says Jessie. The first thing we can do is scratch to the face, head, chest or anything. We can scratch or "rip" ears, as they are sensitive. Biting can be used, especially to a bad person's fingers, arms or legs to help "stun" them to get more time to get away, like in the following examples.

When someone is trying to hurt us or take us away, we do whatever we need to do to get away! ~ Jessie

Eye Gouge and Throat Poke

In addition to scratching and biting, cats go for the eyes. Poking someone in the eye is gross. Pushing our thumbs into someone's eyes to get away is gross. Poking someone in the throat is gross. And we might have to do it anyway to protect ourselves from real danger.

The eyes are a great target if you are up close. If the bad guy or girl cannot see as well, it will be easier for you to escape.
~ Jessie

The throat is a good target because it hurts and makes it hard to breathe. A chop to the throat will only work if it is really hard and you are closer to the bad guy then I am in this picture. Stick to poking the front of the throat, but know this other choice as well in case it is needed. ~ Jessie

Finger Rips

Sometimes in the process of scratching or fighting back, the bad person's fingers become available for biting or ripping.

Remember, like when you bite someone, they get more mad. Be sure after ripping fingers, biting or scratching to run! ~ Jessie

Punching

While we do not encourage punching, because if done incorrectly could lead to broken fingers, knuckles, hands and even arms, we believe making a fist is a natural human defensive thing to do. So we are sharing information on how to do it, yet we strongly recommend the information on palm strikes and hammer fists as safer options to consider. "I really like hammer fists the best," says Jessie.

When punching, remember our power comes from our hips! When we practice that motion described earlier, we can reach further, faster and punch harder. If we have to punch, we use our top two knuckles only. We make sure our thumb is in front of our fist, never on the side or inside our fingers.

Whether we punch with our left or our right hand, we have to remember, chin down (protect it), hip turn, arm extends straight out with slight bend, and the recoil of the arm and hip happen at the same time. Seems hard, but remember, the key is our hips! Oh, did we say that already? Practice, practice, practice!

These pictures demonstrate Jessie making fists then moving into fight position, or as we also call it, our self-defense stance. She can do the same movements you will see with the next technique, palm strikes.

We never put our thumb inside of our fist, never. Bend our knuckles down once, twice, tighten our fist and put the thumb in front of the fingers, only.

~ Dave

Palm Strikes

Palm striking is recommended over punching. When using the bony part on the inside of our palm, below our pinky finger at the bottom of our hand (*not* below our thumb), we are less likely to get hurt. While we will not be able to reach quite as far, it is *very* effective and still powerful. We use the bone at the bottom of our palm under our pinky to the middle of our palm. We must hit with the bone, not the fingers, or we might damage our wrist. So even more than palm strikes, when we can, we use hammer fists to strike the target, which are shown next.

Notice how the hand is slightly cupped, barely turned inward with wrist and fingers tight. "My wrist extends out beyond my fingers so I don't hurt them," Jessie says. The hip motion with this technique is the same as punching. Our wrist is extended and fingers are out of the way.

As you can see with the hip turn and a palm strike, even a little kid like me, who weighs less than 65 pounds, can hurt a big guy! ~ Jessie

Hammer Fist

When making a hammer first, we take the fist that we made to punch with, but instead use the bottom "meaty" portion of the hand (when in a tight fist clenched position). The hammer fist to the front can be used just like a punch. We may not reach as far, but it is very good when someone's nose, head, face or collarbone.

Above you can see me doing a palm strike or a hammer fist. Neither is wrong, just keep doing them until you can escape. ~ Jessie

Elbow Strikes

Lastly, we may need a very powerful elbow to slow the attacker down, because we are, unfortunately, very close. "We use the bony part above, below, or on the "point" of the elbow, when elbowing in all directions, like I pointed out at the front of the book," says Jessie.

It is important to check first to make sure we are about to elbow a bad guy and not grandma or our parents or a little sibling that startled us when coming from out of sight or behind us. Elbows are for when we are close, and we want to be farther away whenever possible so we don't get grabbed. That said, the elbow is a good tool but takes practice to use with any real power. If we are close enough to use an elbow strike, we are too close! We must get away as soon as possible! If we are younger, we try scratching, hammer fists and other techniques more than elbows. All are options for use when we practice and train to use these techniques.

As you can see, I am very close—too close to the bad guy. But if I need to, I can strike with my elbow in many directions. ~ Jessie

Chapter 7: Kicks and Knees

Coach Daddy Dave: What do you like about kicks?

Jessie: I like that they work! Ha ha! And they are fun.

Coach Daddy Dave: What is dangerous about trying to throw knees as a little kid, not a bigger kid like in high school?

Jessie: As you said before, it is dangerous to get too close to the attacker if it is an adult, so kicks are better because you can be farther away. Knees are good sometimes if they person is already on their knees or moving more slowly, because the kick or something else worked first. Kick to the groin and knees!

Kicks and knees can be our greatest tools because we get to use the biggest muscles in our body—the ones in our legs. Kicks are used for longer distances and knees are used up close. As Jessie mentioned correctly above, little kids need to be careful about using knees (or elbows) rather than longer range options because they could be grabbed more easily and taken to the ground. We always want to be on our feet!

When it comes to kicks, these are the ones we believe may be the most effective. When it comes to groin kicks, we are locking our ankle, pointing our toes down and using the top part of the foot where the laces would be in shoes all the way to the middle of the shin bone.

 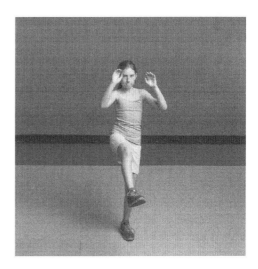

"Remember, when we use our knee, we are using the hard portion of our upper leg, right above the knee cap, but not on the knee cap!" says Jessie.

Look at the difference in distance between Jessie and the bad guy when she is kicking versus using a knee. Be prepared and train to use both, but kick whenever possible. ~ Dave

Often kids and adults are carrying something in their hand, like groceries or a backpack. Look at how I distract the bad guy and push him with the bag. Then when his legs are open because he caught his balance, I can kick and then run! ~ Jessie

Chapter 8: Choke Defenses

Coach Daddy Dave: Chokes are about losing air, and we *need* air! What is the first thing that I taught you about all choke defenses?

Jessie: Tuck your chin down as soon as possible! Tuck your chin!

Coach Daddy Dave: Awesome, what else do you want to say?

Jessie: These are the toughest ones to practice and can be scary, but it is important to know what to do if someone puts their hands around your throat. That is wrong and no one ever should do that to anyone for any reason.

"Tuck your chin! With every choke, we must tuck our chin and move quickly!" Jessie says. It only takes seconds for us to lose our air and pass out, so we need to get the hands off our neck as fast as possible. Tucking our chin to start may get us an extra second or two of oxygen, which is more time to defend ourselves. While there are more chokes we need to know how to defend against, the following are common.

Chokes...Remember, always chin down!

Plucking (Slightly cupping hands & forcefully removing attacker's hands at the thumbs/wrists from any angle)

One Hand Pluck with no Attacker from the Front

 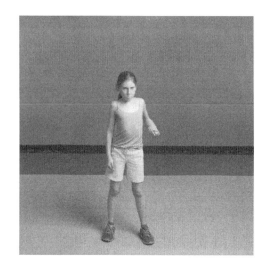

Two Hand Pluck with no Attacker from the Front

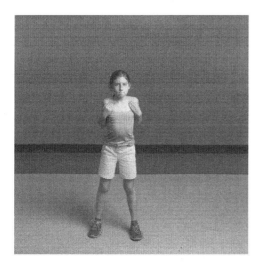
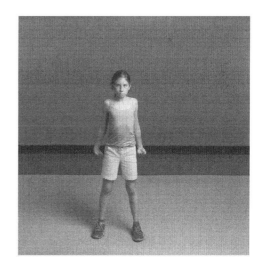

As you can see from a different angle, I cup my hands and slightly raise my arms quickly. When I pull down on the bad guy's thumbs and hands, it's called a pluck. ~ Jessie

Choke Defense from the Side

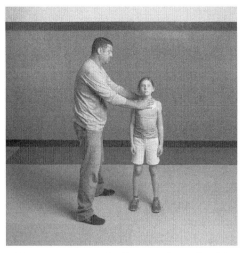 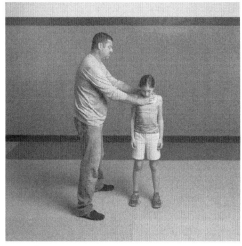

Here someone is choking me from the side. I always first tuck my chin to protect my airway. ~ Jessie

After escaping the side choke or making any defense, consider stomping down on the attacker's toes with your heel like you're smashing a can. ~ Jessie

One-Hand Choke Defense

In these pictures, Jessie decides to break the choke with one hand and strike at the same time. ~ Dave

Two-Hand Choke Defense

Now that I broke his grip on my neck, I can step with my left leg to get balance and kick him in the groin with my right…then run!   ~ Jessie

Chapter 9: Bear Hug Defenses

Coach Daddy Dave: Jessie, why would someone want to put you in a bear hug?

Jessie: Unless it was a friend giving me a hug, the person wanted to either pick me up and throw me or take me away.

Coach Daddy Dave: So what is the most important thing we will need to do when it comes to bear hugs, even if lifted in the air?

Jessie: Separate our hips. I like to practice the bear hug lift from the front and back, then throw an elbow, ha ha. (No longer laughing but sitting on her hands looking innocent). You have to create space so that you can react and kick or knee or do whatever is needed.

What is critical to understand about bear hugs is that the attacker wants to throw or move us. Just like with every choke defense, we tuck our chin. With every bear hug defense, we have to separate the hips. We do this by taking a small step forward with one foot as we lower our body weight. Here are only a few of the ones we need to know.

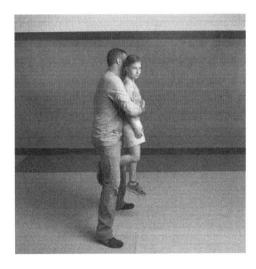

This is when I get a bear hug from behind and get lifted. I bring my heel up on one foot and strike him in the groin. When he drops me, I land and then throw an elbow. Then I run! Even though I'm lifted, I still have to separate my hips. I do this with a kick. ~ Jesse

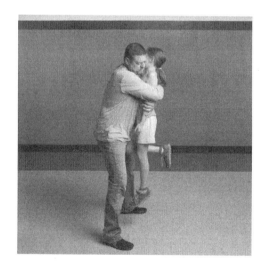

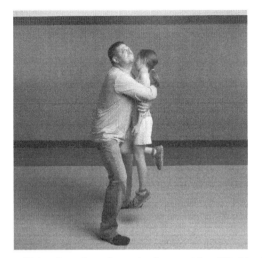

This a bear hug from the front with a lift. I just raise one or two knees fast. When it hits him, I drop. I can then do my strikes before running away. ~ Jessie

After I have landed from being lifted and kneeing the attacker in the groin, when he drops me, I must strike him and then run! ~ Jessie

If I get caught in a bear hug from the front, I do palm strikes to his hips and step a foot back to create space. Then I throw two or three hard, fast knees and hammer fists before running. ~ Jessie

Chapter 10: Hair Pulls

This is something that is common when girls fight one another or if someone wants to move a girl quickly and violently. The self-defense response is also quick and violent, so if we are practicing this move, we need to be very careful or we might damage our training partner's shoulder. It takes almost no energy to hurt our partner or attacker, so we must think about this and be safe!

Coach Daddy Dave: Ahh, hair pulls. You have pretty hair.

Jessie: Thanks, Dad. What's your question? (Smiling, then looking serious)

Coach Daddy Dave: What do you think of these hair pull defenses?

Jessie: I didn't realize there were ways to get out of hair pulls, and now I feel better because I like my long hair. A lot of girls have long hair in the front or the back, so this is a good one for us to know about. I like practicing these, too!

Coach Daddy Dave: Remember, one of the keys to this technique is to drop your chin to your chest after you grab the attacker's hand, then drop your body weight and step back!

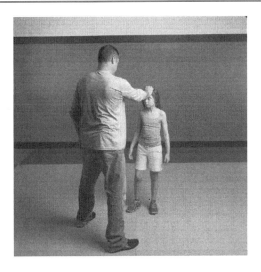 

If someone pulls our hair, the keys are to hold on to the hand that is holding our hair tightly and press it against our forehead by holding the wrist. Then we quickly drop our body towards the ground and step back quickly. This will put the attacker on the floor face down with his or her arm in the air and great pain on the shoulder. It may even rip.

We use the same technique when it is done form the side. Look at the photos below of hair pulls from different directions.

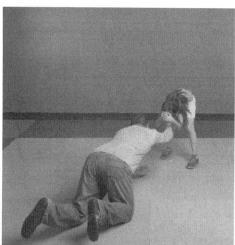
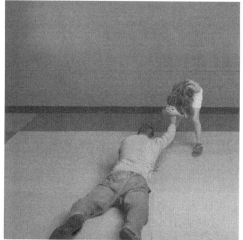

I get his hands at the wrist and push them to my forehead. Then I drop down fast while pulling his arm and stepping back at the same time. Ouch for him! ~ Jessie

Hair Pull from the Side

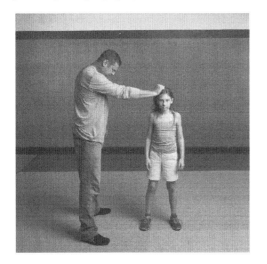 

This is the same thing, only from the side. I turn my head toward him, then I do all the same steps as before. When the bad guy is on the ground, I can run or kick him if he will not let go. ~ Jessie

Hair Pull from Behind

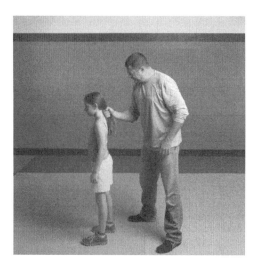 

Getting pulled from behind can really throw off your balance. The key is to make a sweeping step backwards, quickly turn toward the attacker, and strike the groin. Taller kids can turn and strike the face.

The arm and leg move in a "crescent" motion at the same time. Then you follow up with strikes and kicks so you can escape. ~ Dave

Chapter 11: Conclusion

Coach Daddy Dave: Anything else you want to say, Jessie?

Jessie: I will say that this is awesome, and I hope people read our books. There is good stuff in here to help kids *and* adults feel better and safer.

Coach Daddy Dave: Yes, you said it well. This was fun, I love you. Thank you so much.

Jessie: Thank you Daddy, I love you too!

People seem to think it would never happen to them, or if someone attacked, they would end up being nice. We don't believe either to be true. We also believe that based upon statistics, most people that want your stuff, want your stuff. So give it to them! You can replace a cell phone, purse, tablet or other possession. But you are priceless, and no one can replace you.

Listen to and trust your gut. If you must fight to escape, do it and don't give up! In addition to everything covered in this book, there are a lot more skills required to be truly safe, and it all takes practice. We put together the ones we thought we be the most effective and easiest to learn in a short amount of time. Don't forget to find somewhere to train— classes or private lessons—to learn and improve upon these skills with a professional.

We hope you enjoyed this book on how to defend yourself when standing up. We hope you will consider learning some skills that will help you when someone is trying to hurt you when you're on the ground. Find those in our second daddy-daughter L.I.F.E. Line book on kids' ground techniques and more.

Grab on to L.I.F.E. Line Self-Defense™!

With love,
Jessie and Dave

"Always chase your dreams instead of running from your fears."
~Unknown

Next in the L.I.F.E. Line Self-Defense™ *Series*

L.I.F.E. Line Self-Defense™:
Kids' Ground Techniques and More

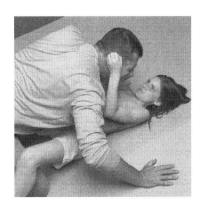

L.I.F.E. Line Self-Defense™:
Graduation, College Bound and Beyond!

About Jessie Gerber

As a ten year old, there are few people who really get to know someone at such a young age. However, as most kids can appreciate, having a good sitter to stay with when parents are away is priceless. Here is what Jessie's long time "Girl Sitters" had to say:

"When I first met Jessie, she was a cheerful and adorable six month old. I was hired as her first babysitter, but the Gerbers quickly became family to me. Jessie is positive, thoughtful, determined, and mature beyond her years. I am not surprised in the least that she is working on her first book! I am excited for all of her future projects and adventures. Go Jessie!" ~ Maggie

"I met Jessie a couple years ago, and she has never failed to have a smile on her face. From the moment I met her, I knew she had a warm heart and a positive attitude. She will brighten up whatever room she is in.I cannot wait to see what the future holds for her, as I know she will be a strong, independent young lady!" ~ Sarah

"Jessie is the most talented nine year old. She loves to read, play the piano, plays multiple sports and even speaks Spanish. She never seems to give up, and if something comes along and slows her down, she learns from it to come back even stronger. Jessie always has smile on her face and is willing to help anyone as much as she can. Jessie is simply awesome!" ~ Brittney

"Jessie's positive attitude makes her shine in any situation. Her passion and enthusiasm for everything she does contributes to her energetic nature, always striving to do her best." ~ Ashley

Jessie Leah Gerber has shown impressive willingness to learn, be reflective, communicate and support the world as she learns and grows. She is an avid fan of ice skating, yet she has participated in many activities in order to try new experiences. Jessie enjoys playing with her puppy (Freedom), the piano, riding her bike, drawing, shooting baskets, the outdoors, gardens and more.

Jessie has participated in many L.I.F.E. Line Self-Defense demonstrations with her dad and is always curious about learning more. She started Tae Kwon Do at the age of three and loved doing "Daddy Dojo," where she began her Krav Maga journey with her father. Jessie's favorite part was getting to beat on her dad who ended up needing to wear protective gear and a mouth guard very early on!

Jessie has also recorded a song, which she performed in front of 50 people in a live audience singing a Capella. She has tried everything from gymnastics to soccer to lacrosse and more. She is recognized by those who meet her as fun, caring, empathetic, and ahead of her time.

She is a natural leader with a very bright future!

About Dave Gerber

Dave Gerber is President and founder of Synergy Development & Training, LLC, an innovative organizational solutions company, that specializes in helping businesses, government agencies, organizations, schools and individuals use conflict as an opportunity to increase performance, revenue and reduce risk.

Dave helps individuals understand the impact of conflict at work. He specializes in motivating others to increase and actualize their new professional and personal potential. He also loves being such a huge role in Jessie's life. Dave has included her on many types of cool projects like these two books.

As a leader, coach, trainer, author and motivational speaker, he has worked with business owners, managers, employees of all kinds, CEOs, military officers, project managers, sales leaders, doctors, lawyers, engineers, educators and many more. He has hands-on experience working with thousands of training participants and students of all ages, races, backgrounds and ability levels. His passionate and motivating style is contagious. Dave has worked with over 10,000 individuals of all kinds.

Dave is also a Krav Maga instructor and practitioner, along with being a Knife Instructor. While he has not been a lifelong martial artist, he has been a lifelong educator. Now he has combined the two.

Some of Dave's background in Krav Maga and Self-Defense includes:

- Certified Krav Maga Instructor: Alpha Krav Maga International (AKMI) Expert I
- Alpha Krav Maga International Leadership Program Director
- Owner and Head Coach of Alpha Krav Maga International Northern Virginia/DC Metro
- Certified Full Knife Instructor: Patriot Martial Arts, San Antonio, TX
- Holds Practitioner Certificates with: Alpha Krav Maga International, Krav Maga World Wide and the IMI System (tested in Israel)

www.Akminvadc.com

www.davegerber.info

www.synergydt.com

www.synergy-selfdefense.com

www.kravmaga.vet

Sources Consulted

Content for the book comes from Dave's ongoing notes, instructor training notes, instructor training curriculum, listening and training, best practices and lessons learned from the following individuals over the course Dave's education and travels while studying Krav Maga from many systems. He has also read thousands of pages of text, countless articles, and web postings, and he has watched hundreds of videos.

That said, none of them were viewed or reviewed while making this project. Everything included is how he was taught over the last six years, instructor trainings and from his personal writings. The following are responsible for the bulk of Dave's training efforts and deserve recognition:

- Sam Sade (Former Israeli Military & Alpha Krav Maga International Owner, 4th Dan Black Belt in Krav Maga, Martial Arts Hall of Fame) and Alpha Krav Maga Curriculum

- George Buruian, Martial Arts Masters Hall of Fame

- Marcus Kowal (Internationally Known, Systems Training Center, 2nd Dan Black Belt, former lead for KMWW in LA)

- Former Instructors at Krav Maga NVA

- Yossi Schmueli (Former Police Officer and Level 4 IMI Instructor, Tal Shahar, Israel)

- Systems that Dave has trained with and studied in particular are the Krav Maga systems of:

  - Alpha Krav Maga International

  - Krav Maga World Wide

  - IMI System (Israel)

Testimonials from Community Leaders

"As a parent, I can think of few things more important than ensuring that my daughter can protect herself as she goes out into the world after graduation. Dave Gerber's techniques in self-defense are just the tools young women need to feel empowered to take care of themselves should they ever feel threatened or endangered. His energizing, direct approach to teaching hundreds of girls at the high school assembly was great to watch. Every school should do this program!"

> ~ SP (PTA Leader)

"I spend my time healing people, so I don't like violence. That said, if someone is being attacked, they should know how to defend themselves. Kids are no different. Your program and book is a must have for the collection in every home. I really like the L.I.F.E. Line concept, as it underscores the need to pursue problem solving before physical contact, but is realistic about the need for safety and survival skills. Fantastic!"

> ~ Dr. TW (Surgeon)

"We need our kids to be ready for the future, period. Safety is a part of that, and you two have created something that is special and will help people of all ages, not just kids. Great job!"

> ~ Retired Colonel TM (Retired U.S. Military Officer)

"I saw Dave Gerber in action as he motivated, empowered and taught basic self-defense skills to 500 young ladies at our high school. After just 30 minutes in what felt like an amazing pep rally, they learned the importance of situational awareness and some techniques in order to defend themselves. They clearly walked away wanting to learn more, which is not surprising given Dave's talent as a teacher and a coach. I would highly suggest that *every* high school do this program in order to help better prepare their girls for life now and after graduation!"

> ~ JT (PTA Leader)